HAL LEONARD STUDENT

Rhythm Wi
The Blues

A Comprehensive Rhythm Program for Musicians

TABLE OF CONTENTS

ISBN-13: 978-0-634-08803-2
ISBN-10: 0-634-08803-3

HAL•LEONARD®
CORPORATION

7777 W. BLUEMOUND RD. P.O. BOX 13819 MILWAUKEE, WI 53213

Visit Hal Leonard Online at
www.halleonard.com

A Note to Students

Welcome to *Rhythm Without the Blues* – Volume One. This unique program will take you from the very basics of rhythm to an advanced level of comprehension and performance ability. The materials in your workbook, combined with practice exercises and demonstrations on the CD, work together to bring a clear understanding of the basics of rhythm. The demonstrations, exercises and dictations will give you the necessary practice so that you will be equipped to understand and perform a vast array of rhythmic patterns.

You will find this series easy to use. To use the books effectively, you will need a metronome and a CD player.

Each chapter is divided into smaller sections. This allows you to focus on one section for a short period of time. Working in small sections is more valuable than trying to cover large amounts of material. Learning this way lays a good foundation as you continue to build your skills.

All exercises and dictations may be used repeatedly for additional practice or review. For written exercises, you may either erase your answers or use a separate sheet of paper.

YOUR CD:
- You may access tracks on your CD by moving from smaller numbers up or from larger numbers down. Simply press the track buttons to find the desired track number.
- ▶▶| • This button will move forward through the CD.
- |◀◀ • This button will move backward through the CD. Larger numbers may easily be reached by moving backward from Track 1 while the CD is playing.
- The dictations and exercises are played once. Repeat tracks as many times as necessary to complete each exercise.

YOUR WORKBOOK:

METROMONE: This program requires the use of a metronome, so let's discuss this first.

In 1816, a man by the name of Maelzel manufactured a mechanical device which sounded an adjustable number of beats per minute. Whenever a composer wants the speed or tempo of their piece to be fixed at a certain number of beats per minute—let's say 60, for example—they will write M.M. plus the symbol for a note equals 60, just as you see in the box on the next page. The M.M. stands for Maelzel's Metronome. The number 60 simply indicates that the metronome will beat 60 times per minute. In your workbook, the symbol for the metronome is shown as a bell as seen on the next page.

Metronome speed is indicated like this:

🔔 M.M. ♩ = 60

This is how it will be shown throughout this series.

Take some time to consult the manual for your metronome and familiarize yourself with its operation and how it sounds at different settings.

The metronome sound is given to help you establish a standard by which to judge the rhythmic pattern. Each bell represents one pulse or beat of the metronome.

On the CD, you will hear the metronome give a count-off before every exercise or dictation. This will prepare you for the beginning of the exercise or dictation.

NOTATION

You will notice that only the stems of the notes are being used, as indicated below:

| ⊓

Noteheads will only be shown when they are needed to indicate the time value of the rhythm. This will become clear as you progress through the book.

HEADINGS

All of the chapters are set up in the same way. Headings appear on the left-hand side of the page. These headings introduce a series of tasks designed to familiarize you with various rhythmic patterns. Headings include NEW ELEMENT, LISTENING, TAPPING, MATCHING, and DICTATION.

NEW ELEMENT

LISTENING

TAPPING

MATCHING

DICTATION

NEW ELEMENT

Under this heading, you will see a large subdivided table. The first section of the table, **Rhythm**, shows what the rhythm symbol looks like. The second section, **Term**, gives the technical name. The third section, **Value**, tells how many beats that rhythm is worth. In the last section, **Rhythm Name**, a spoken syllable is assigned to that rhythm. See the example below.

Rhythm	Term	Value	Rhythm Name
|	quarter	one beat	ta

LISTENING

Under this heading, you will be given an opportunity to listen to what the rhythm sounds like on the CD. In the example, you will hear two sounds: (1) the metronome and (2) an instrument sounding the rhythmic pattern on a single pitch.

The example will be demonstrated first. You will then have a chance to practice tapping the example. To tap rhythms, strike the tips of your fingers on the edge of a table, palm facing down. Following this, a musical example containing the new element will usually be heard.

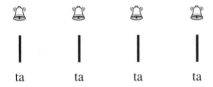

TAPPING

Material under this heading presents you with an opportunity to practice the new element without the CD.

You will use your metronome to help keep a steady beat. The metronome marking is indicated beside the heading. Set your metronome to the tempo shown.

You will want to learn to feel the basic beat by tapping it yourself. Begin tapping an even beat, equivalent to the metronome, with the hand opposite the one with which you will be tapping the rhythmic patterns. If you are right-handed, you will probably be tapping the rhythms with your right hand and the metronome beat with your left hand. When you have established a steady beat with one hand, begin tapping the rhythmic patterns with the other hand. At first it might feel like rubbing your head and patting your stomach at the same time, but as you persevere, it will become more and more natural for you.

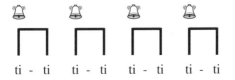

MATCHING

Under this heading, you will see a series of boxes containing rhythmic patterns. Here you will match the patterns you hear on the CD, in correct sequence, by indicating the corresponding letters in the spaces provided.

❘ ❘	⊓ ⊓
A	**B**
❘ ⊓	⊓ ❘
C	**D**

1. _____   2. _____

3. _____   4. _____

DICTATION

The next heading contains a series of exercises in which you will write down the rhythmic patterns that you hear.

Only the stems of rhythmic patterns will be used. This is a form of rhythmic shorthand which will help as you write the dictations. Develop your own shorthand in dictations. For example, if you need to write a series of notes that are joined at the top, simply write the basic outline and fill it in later. This will become easier as you progress.

On the CD, you will hear each dictation once. Repeat the tracks as often as necessary to complete each exercise.

- First, listen and tap along with the metronome. Listen closely for the rhythmic pattern associated with each beat.

- Speak the rhythm name associated with each pattern, for example, *ti-ti* or *ta*. You may want to do this more than once.

- Next, begin to fill in the patterns under the metronome symbols using the rhythmic shorthand. Write in as many patterns as you can remember each time.

1.   2.

Remember, with the exercises and dictations, it is accuracy that counts. Speed will come later.

You and your teacher may want to chart your progress. Try keeping a log showing the number of times you had to listen to the exercises before completing them and how accurately you were able to tap exercises the first time.

We recommend that you use the companion series:

Ear Without Fear

Ear Without Fear is a comprehensive ear-training program. Using these two series together will help you to master the dictations and exercises in Levels 2, 3, and 4 with success.

A Note to Teachers

Rhythm Without the Blues is an innovative program aimed at building a clear understanding of rhythm and the ability to perform it accurately.

Rhythm is a complex task that is mathematical in structure. It is distinct from ear training, which has a melodic component and employs different neurological pathways, yet both elements are invariably placed together in music training. The result is often frustration and a sense of failure. Ultimately, these elements will be combined. However, in Volume 1, rhythm is presented independently. Levels 2, 3, and 4 provide exercises that integrate rhythmic and melodic components.

Educators have long known that step-by-step learning is essential. A sense of accomplishment and confidence at each level is the motivating force behind the desire to continue. It is assumed at the beginning of Volume 1 that the student may have no prior experience with rhythm. Therefore, the first three chapters cover the basics. Some students, particularly those who have studied an instrument, may have already developed an understanding of these concepts. However, the balance of the book offers demonstrations, listening, performance opportunities, and rhythmic dictations which will help even experienced students to reinforce and hone rhythmic skills.

We have carefully chosen and organized the materials in this book to make the learning process as accessible to students as possible. The Workbook and the CD are integrated to provide several learning approaches: AURAL, VISUAL, and PRACTICAL. Together, they present a comprehensive, step-by-step learning program for which the student can assume primary responsibility.

The following concepts will be covered in Volume 1:

- note and rest recognition
- time signatures $\frac{2}{4}$ and $\frac{3}{4}$
- note and rest groupings in the two time signatures
- demonstrations, exercises, and dictations covering these areas
- instruction in the use of the metronome

Stems will be used to indicate time values. Noteheads are not used unless the notehead indicates the value of that rhythm. This enables the student to focus solely on the rhythmic elements. Rhythm names will be used to facilitate recognition of rhythmic elements. The rhythm names used have been adapted from those developed and advanced by Emile-Joseph Chevé, John Curwen, Zoltán Kodály, and Pierre Perron.

- It provides a prepared curriculum.

- Students can work independently with well-formatted, easily understood materials.

- Chapters are easily subdivided for appropriately-sized weekly assignments.

- Exercises and dictations are readily available for weekly testing and instruction.

- Lesson time is maximized for instrument instruction, while ensuring that the student is honing musicianship skills.

Students often find the development of essential rhythmic and aural skills less exciting than learning an instrument, so a reward system may be helpful. Consider implementing one, using some of the following suggestions:

- Encourage students to keep a log, outlining the number of sections and exercises completed over the week. They may also want to keep track of how long it takes to complete each exercise. Students' confidence will grow as they begin to see an increase in proficiency and speed.

- Award incentive points for successful completion of sections and increased proficiency. Give prizes and awards based on accumulated points.

It is recommended that students also use the companion series:

Ear Without Fear

Ear Without Fear is a comprehensive ear-training program that works in tandem with *Rhythm Without the Blues.* Using them together will greatly enhance the ability of the student to master the dictations and exercises contained in each series successfully.

CHAPTER 1

Quarter and eighth notes:

In the first half of this chapter, the new element is the QUARTER NOTE, worth one beat with the rhythm name *ta*.

NEW ELEMENT

Rhythm	Term	Value	Rhythm Name
|	quarter	one beat	ta

Now let's go on to the next heading box marked LISTENING. Here you will be given an opportunity to listen to what the rhythm sounds like. Before the pattern in Example A begins, the metronome will beat four times by itself. This will prepare you for the beginning of the pattern. In the example, you will hear three sounds: (1) the metronome, (2) the instrument sounding the rhythmic pattern on a single note and (3) the voice speaking "ta" on the rhythmic pattern along with the instrument.

Throughout the series, this symbol 🔔 indicates one beat of the metronome.

 **LISTENING**   PLAY CD TRACK 1

TAPPING   Throughout the book, always set your metronome to 🔔 = 60 and turn it on. Tap the rhythms while speaking the rhythm names.

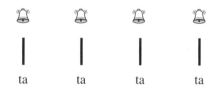

To tap rhythms, strike the tips of your fingers on the edge of a table, palm facing down.

Most chapters contain only one new element, some contain two. Chapter 1 has two new elements and we will now go on to discover the second. Then we will put these two new elements together to make some interesting and different rhythmic patterns.

NEW ELEMENT

Please study the NEW ELEMENT table carefully. You will see that our new element is called *ti-ti* and is made up of two EIGHTH NOTES with the stems joined together by a single beam across the top.

Rhythm is really applied mathematics. One and one must always make two. Since an eighth note is equal to half the value of a quarter note, it therefore makes mathematical sense, as well as musical sense, to say that two eighth notes equal one quarter note.

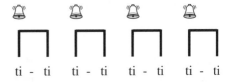

The two eighth notes must be played or sounded evenly in the same space of time that a quarter note is played or sounded. Therefore, when you hear the metronome sounding one beat, you will hear two evenly spaced notes indicating *ti-ti*.

Rhythm	Term	Value	Rhythm Name
⊓	two eighths	one beat	ti-ti

LISTENING   PLAY CD TRACK 2

ti - ti   ti - ti   ti - ti   ti - ti

TAPPING   🔔 M.M. ♩ = 60

Tap the rhythmic pattern and speak the rhythm name.

ti - ti   ti - ti   ti - ti   ti - ti

11

Quarter (*ta*) and eighth (*ti-ti*) notes can be put together in several ways to produce different rhythms.

 **LISTENING**   PLAY CD TRACK 3

ta   ti - ti   ti - ti   ta

 PLAY CD TRACK 4

Franz Joseph Haydn (1732-1809) wrote the Surprise Symphony. Listen to the following musical example from this work, which demonstrates the use of *ti-ti* and *ta*.

ti - ti   ti - ti   ti - ti   ta   ti - ti   ti - ti   ti - ti   ta   ti - ti   ti - ti   ti - ti   ta   ti - ti   ti - ti   ta   ta

TAPPING   🔔 M.M. ♩ = 60

For each of the following exercises, tap the rhythmic pattern and speak the rhythm names.

1.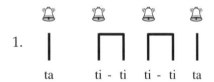

ta   ti - ti   ti - ti   ta

2.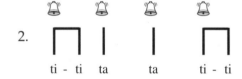

ti - ti   ta   ta   ti - ti

3.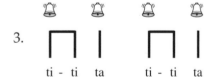

ti - ti   ta   ti - ti   ta

4.

ti - ti   ti - ti   ta   ti - ti

MATCHING

Using the rhythm boxes below, find the rhythms that match the exercises on CD tracks 5–8. Each exercise uses two rhythm boxes and will be played twice. Write the letters of the corresponding boxes in the spaces provided. If you need to hear the exercises again, simply repeat the track. Answers are on page 49.

PLAY CD TRACKS 5–8

Remember to listen for the four strikes of the metronome that will precede each exercise.

A

B

C

D

1. _____   2. _____

3. _____   4. _____

DICTATION

Play the tracks one at a time. Under the given metronome symbols, write the rhythmic patterns that you hear. If you need to hear the exercise again, simply repeat the track. Answers are on page 49.

PLAY CD TRACKS 9–12

If there is more than one stem in a rhythmic pattern, as in ti-ti, the first stem of the pattern must be placed directly under the metronome symbol. See pages 10 and 11 for examples.

1.

2.

3.

4.

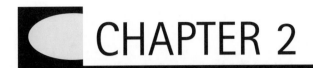

CHAPTER 2

Quarter rest: 𝄽

NEW ELEMENT

Rhythm	Term	Value	Rhythm Name
𝄽	quarter rest	one beat	rest

A REST means that no note or sound is played for the duration of the rest. Like the quarter note, the QUARTER REST has a time value of one beat. When you are tapping a rhythm and come to a quarter rest, instead of tapping, turn your hand with your palm facing upward to indicate one beat.

A rest is a beat of silence. A quarter rest has the same value as a quarter note.

$$𝄽 = |$$

You will notice that the metronome continues to mark the beat for the duration of the rest. Remember to hold your palm face upward while the metronome sounds one beat.

LISTENING   PLAY CD TRACK 13

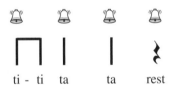

PLAY CD TRACK 14

Here is an example of the quarter rest in the children's tune "Twinkle, Twinkle Little Star."

TAPPING   🔔 M.M. ♩ = 60

For each of the following exercises, tap the rhythmic pattern and speak the rhythm names.

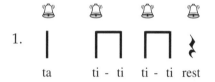

1.

ta   ti - ti   ti - ti rest

2.

ta   rest   ti - ti ta

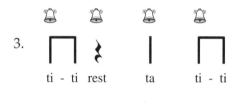

3.

ti - ti rest   ta   ti - ti

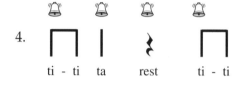

4.

ti - ti ta   rest   ti - ti

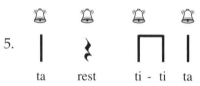

5.

ta   rest   ti - ti ta

MATCHING

Using the rhythm boxes, find the rhythms that match the exercises. Each exercise uses two rhythm boxes and will be played twice before going on to the next rhythm. Write the letters of the corresponding boxes in the spaces provided. If you need to hear the exercises again, simply repeat the track. Answers are on page 49.

PLAY CD TRACK 15

A	B	C
D	E	F

1. _____   2. _____   3. _____   4. _____

To draw a quarter rest, begin by writing a "z". Z

Then without lifting your pencil, write a "c" directly underneath. Zᴄ

Using these examples as a guide, practice drawing quarter rests in the space below.

DICTATION

Play the CD tracks one at a time. Write the rhythmic patterns that you hear under the given metronome symbols. Repeat the track as many times as necessary to finish the dictations. Answers are on page 49.

PLAY CD TRACKS 16–19

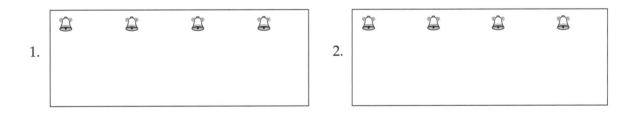

1.

2.

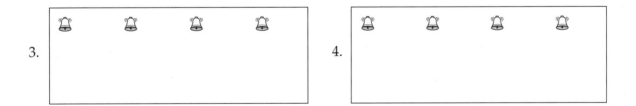

3.

4.

Accuracy should be achieved in three out of four dictations before proceeding to the next chapter.

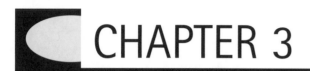

CHAPTER 3

Bar lines and the time signatures $\frac{2}{4}$ and $\frac{3}{4}$

NEW ELEMENT

Beats are organized into groups. Each group of beats is contained in the space between two bar lines called a MEASURE (or BAR). A long vertical line shows the end of each measure and is called a BAR LINE. A DOUBLE BAR LINE indicates the end of the music or rhythm, as in the diagram below.

The number of beats each measure contains is indicated by the TIME SIGNATURE, which is placed at the beginning of the music or rhythmic pattern.

A time signature is made up of two numbers. The top number indicates how many beats will be in each measure. The bottom number shows what kind of note will get one beat. These two values, represented by the time signature are referred to as the METER. So, in the following example, the 2 indicates that there are two beats per measure and the 4 represents a quarter note. This means that there will be the equivalent of two quarter notes in every measure.

Another way to think of it is like this:

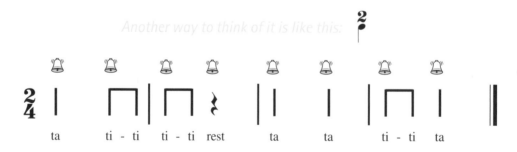

In $\frac{2}{4}$ meter, there is a natural accent or emphasis on the first beat of each bar, making the second beat weaker in contrast. Listen to the following example of $\frac{2}{4}$ meter.

LISTENING   PLAY CD TRACK 20

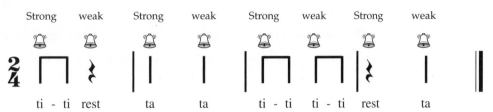

PLAY CD TRACK 21

"Die Forelle" ("The Trout") by Austrian composer Franz Schubert (1797-1828) is a good
example of $\frac{2}{4}$ meter. Listen for the strong and weak beats.

TAPPING   M.M. ♩ = 60

**For each of the following exercises, tap the rhythmic pattern and speak
the rhythm names.**

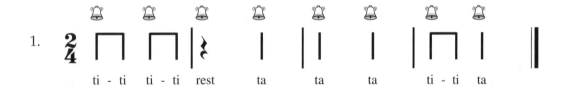

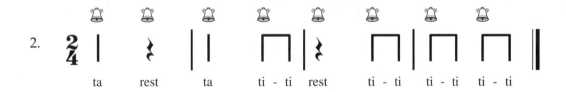

MATCHING

Play the CD tracks one at a time. Once again, match the given rhythmic patterns to the boxes shown below, placing them in correct order in the spaces provided. Each exercise now uses four rhythm boxes and is played twice. Remember to keep repeating the track until each exercise has been completed. Answers are on page 49.

PLAY CD TRACK 22

As we are now in 2/4 meter, remember to listen first for the two strikes of the metronome that will precede each exercise.

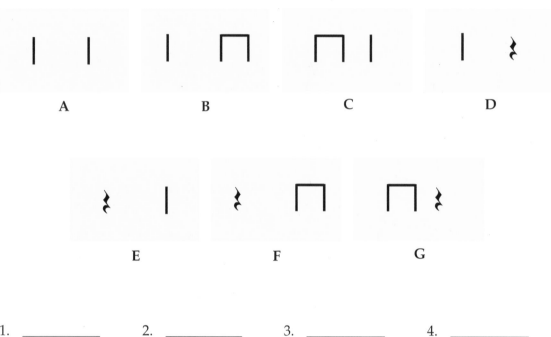

1. _____   2. _____   3. _____   4. _____

NEW ELEMENT

Here is a new time signature, ¾. The 3 indicates three beats per measure, and the 4 represents a quarter note. This means that there will be the equivalent of three quarter notes in every bar.

Another way to think of it is like this: ♩³

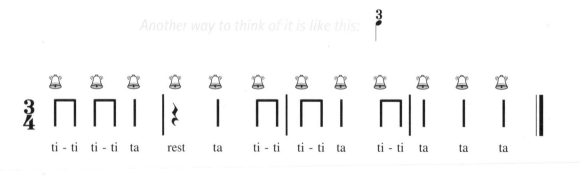

LISTENING PLAY CD TRACK 23

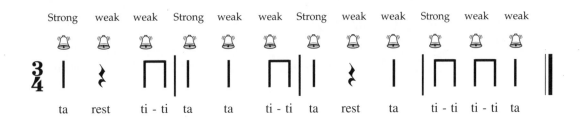

As in $\frac{2}{4}$ time, there is a natural accent or emphasis on the first beat of each bar.

The last two beats are weaker by contrast. Waltzes are in $\frac{3}{4}$ time.

PLAY CD TRACK 24

Listen for the "Strong, weak, weak" in "On the Beautiful Blue Danube" by Viennese composer Johann Strauss Jr. (1825-1899).

TAPPING   M.M. ♩ = 60

For each of the following exercises, tap the rhythmic pattern and speak the rhythm names

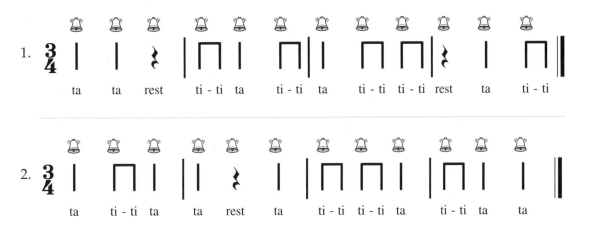

21

MATCHING

Match the given rhythmic patterns to the boxes shown below, placing them in correct order in the spaces provided. Each exercise is made up of four rhythmic patterns and is played twice. Answers are on page 49.

PLAY CD TRACK 25

As we are now in $\frac{3}{4}$ meter, remember to listen first for the three strikes of the metronome that will precede each exercise.

A

B

C

D

E

F

5. _____   6. _____   7. _____   8. _____

Remember that from now on you will be using two different time signatures, so you will need to observe which one is being used. In $\frac{2}{4}$ meter, two beats of the metronome will sound before the dictation begins. In $\frac{3}{4}$ meter, three beats of the metronome will sound.

DICTATION

Play the CD tracks one at a time. Write the rhythmic pattern that you hear under the given metronome symbols. Repeat the track as many times as necessary to finish the dictation. Answers are on page 49.

PLAY CD TRACKS 26–29

1. $\frac{3}{4}$

2. $\frac{2}{4}$

3. $\frac{3}{4}$

4. $\frac{2}{4}$

Half note and dotted half note: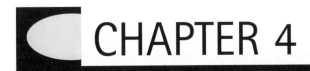

NEW ELEMENT

Rhythm	Term	Value	Rhythm Name
♩ (half note)	half	two beats	ta - a

Our new rhythmic element, the HALF NOTE, gives us an opportunity to listen for a held (sustained) note. There will only be a subtle difference between this note and what a quarter note sounds like, followed by a rest. The half note sounds for two full beats.

The *ta-a* symbol is made up of one stem with a hollow notehead. This represents a half note. A half note has the value of two quarter notes.

$$\text{♩} = \text{|} \quad \text{|}$$

When tapping, we need to distinguish between a half note and a quarter note followed by a rest. To indicate the half note, hold your hand palm down for two beats. A quarter note followed by a rest will be indicated by tapping the quarter note palm down and then turning your palm up for the quarter rest.

 LISTENING   PLAY CD TRACK 30

 PLAY CD TRACK 31

In the song "Amazing Grace," you will hear the use of the half note.

TAPPING  M.M. ♩ = 60

For each of the following exercises, tap the rhythmic pattern and speak the rhythm names.

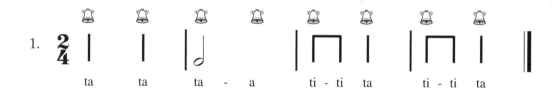

1. **2/4** | | | ♩ | | | | | |
ta   ta   ta - a   ti - ti   ta   ti - ti   ta

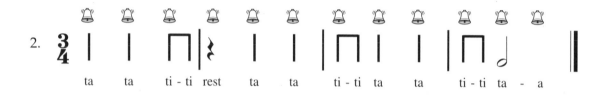

2. **3/4**
ta   ta   ti - ti   rest   ta   ta   ti - ti   ta   ta   ti - ti   ta - a

3. **2/4**
ta - a   ti - ti   ti - ti   ta   ti - ti   ti - ti   rest

4. **3/4**
ta   ti - ti   rest   ti - ti   ti - ti   ta   ta - a   ti - ti   ti - ti   ta   ti - ti

5. **2/4**
ti - ti   ta   ta - a   rest   ti - ti   ta   ti - ti

NEW ELEMENT

Rhythm	Term	Value	Rhythm Name
	dotted half	three beats	ta - a - a

Our next rhythmic element is the DOTTED HALF NOTE. The dotted half note is held (sustained) for three full beats.

When a dot is placed after any rhythm, it adds exactly half the value of that rhythm. Since a half note equals two beats, the dot equals one beat, and they combine to make three beats.

$$\text{♩.} = |\ \ |\ \ |$$

LISTENING   PLAY CD TRACK 32

ta   ti - ti rest   ta - a - a   ti - ti ta - a   ti - ti ti - ti ta

PLAY CD TRACK 33

This tune demonstrates the dotted half note.

ta - a - a   ta - a - a   ta - a - a

The song "Edelweiss" from Rodgers' and Hammerstein's *The Sound of Music* also demonstrates the dotted half note.

TAPPING

M.M. ♩ = 60

For each of the following exercises, tap the rhythmic pattern and speak the rhythm names.

1. **3/4** ti - ti ti - ti rest ta - a - a ti - ti ti - ti ta ta ta - a

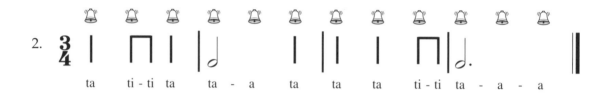

2. **3/4** ta ti - ti ta ta - a ta ta ta ti - ti ta - a - a

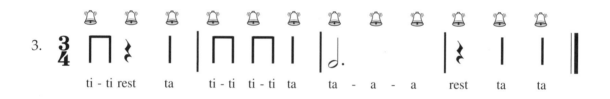

3. **3/4** ti - ti rest ta ti - ti ti - ti ta ta - a - a rest ta ta

4. **3/4** ta - a - a ta ti - ti ta ti - ti ta - a ti - ti rest ta

5. **3/4** ta - a ti - ti ta - a - a ti - ti ta ta ta ti - ti ti - ti

MATCHING

Match the given rhythmic patterns to the boxes shown below, placing them in correct order in the spaces provided. Each exercise is made up of four rhythmic patterns and is played twice. Answers are on page 50.

PLAY CD TRACK 34

These exercises are in $\frac{2}{4}$ meter.

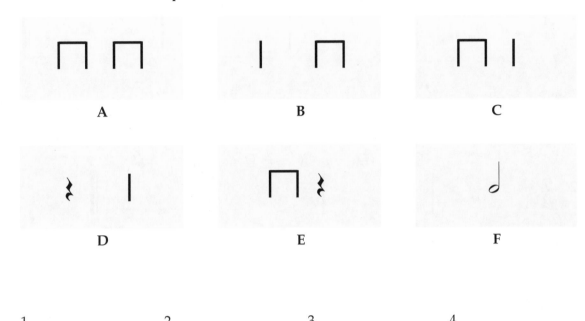

A   B   C

D   E   F

1. _____   2. _____   3. _____   4. _____

PLAY CD TRACK 35

These exercises are in $\frac{3}{4}$ meter.

A   B   C

D   E   F

5. _____   6. _____   7. _____   8. _____

DICTATION

Play the tracks one at a time. Write the rhythmic pattern that you hear under the given metronome symbols. Repeat the track if necessary. Answers are on page 50.

 PLAY CD TRACKS 36–39

1. $\frac{3}{4}$

2. $\frac{2}{4}$

3. $\frac{3}{4}$

4. $\frac{2}{4}$

CHAPTER 5

Dotted quarter-eighth note: ♩. ♪

NEW ELEMENT

Rhythm	Term	Value	Rhythm Name
♩. ♪	dotted quarter, 1 eighth	two beats	tam – ti

In this chapter, we will be learning the *tam-ti*, which introduces us to the DOTTED QUARTER NOTE. As we discussed in Chapter 4, a dot after a note increases the value by one half.

In *tam-ti*, the dot following the quarter equals an eighth note. The single eighth note is made up of a stem with a FLAG (tail) on the right side. The dotted quarter note and eighth note combine to equal two beats.

$$♩. \quad ♪ \quad = \quad | \quad |$$

LISTENING PLAY CD TRACK 40

PLAY CD TRACK 41

The "Hallelujah Chorus" from G.F. Handel's (1685-1759) *Messiah* gives us a clear example of the *tam-ti*.

TAPPING

🔔 M.M. ♩ = 60

For each of the following exercises, tap the rhythmic pattern with one hand and the metronome beat with the opposite hand.

1.
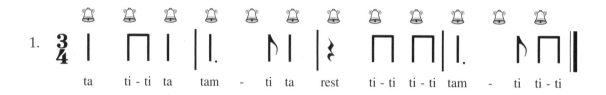

ta   ti - ti   ta   tam - ti   ta   rest   ti - ti   ti - ti   tam - ti   ti - ti

2.

tam - ti   ta   ti - ti   ti - ti   ta   rest   ta

3.
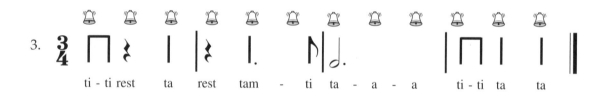

ti - ti rest   ta   rest   tam - ti   ta - a - a   ti - ti   ta   ta

4.
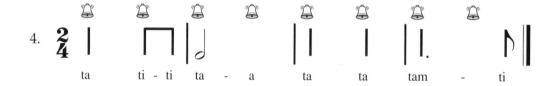

ta   ti - ti   ta - a   ta   ta   tam - ti

MATCHING

Match the given rhythmic patterns to the boxes shown below, placing them in correct order in the spaces provided. Each example is made up of four rhythmic patterns and is played twice. Answers are on page 50.

PLAY CD TRACK 42

These exercises are in $\frac{2}{4}$ meter.

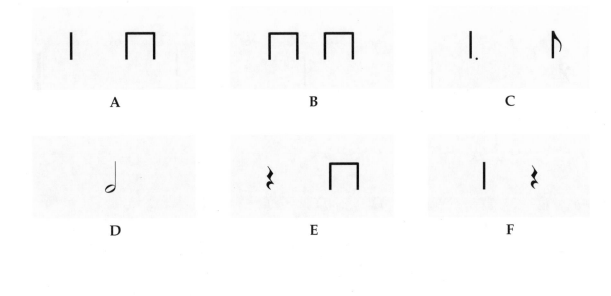

1. _____   2. _____   3. _____   4. _____

PLAY CD TRACKS 43

These exercises are in $\frac{3}{4}$ meter.

5. _____   6. _____   7. _____   8. _____

DICTATION

Play the tracks one at a time. Write the rhythmic pattern that you hear under the given metronome symbols. Answers are on page 50.

PLAY CD TRACKS 44–47

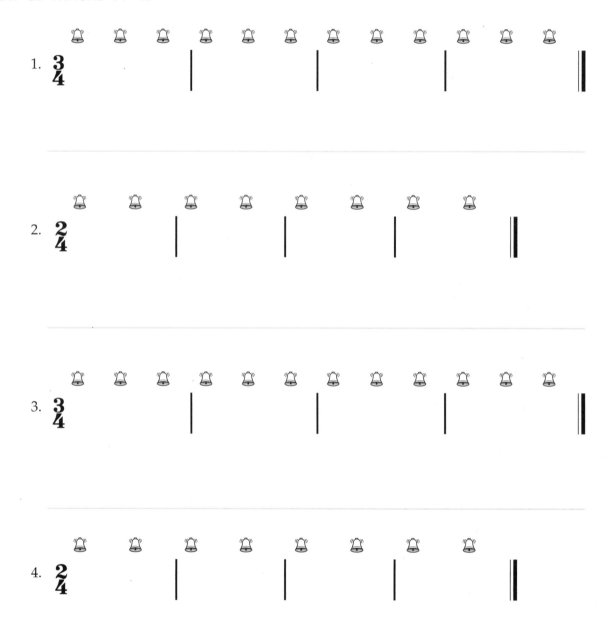

CHAPTER 6

Traditional counting

We already know that a time signature of $\frac{2}{4}$ indicates there will be the equivalent of two quarter notes in every measure. It is often useful to know which beat, or part of a beat you are on in relation to the entire measure. Traditional counting helps to divide the beats.

Numbers are used to indicate the main beats.

The main beat is the quarter note. In $\frac{2}{4}$ meter, the quarter notes are counted as: *one, two*.

In $\frac{3}{4}$ meter, the quarter notes are counted as: *one, two, three*.

The word "and" is used to divide the beat. This will allow us to count the eighth notes when they appear.

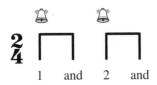

Here the beat is divided. The number represents the first half of the beat. The "and" comes on the second half of the beat.

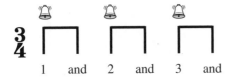

Counting shorthand: "1 and 2 and" becomes "1 + 2 +."

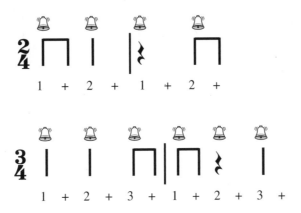

LISTENING PLAY CD TRACK 48

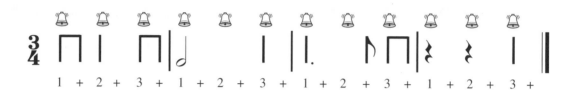

1 + 2 + 3 + 1 + 2 + 3 + 1 + 2 + 3 + 1 + 2 + 3 +

TAPPING M.M. ♩ = 60

For each of the following exercises, tap the rhythmic pattern with one hand while speaking the traditional counting.

1. **2/4**

1 + 2 + 1 + 2 + 1 + 2 + 1 + 2 +

2. **3/4**

1 + 2 + 3 + 1 + 2 + 3 + 1 + 2 + 3 + 1 + 2 + 3 +

3. **2/4**

1 + 2 + 1 + 2 + 1 + 2 + 1 + 2 +

4. **3/4**

1 + 2 + 3 + 1 + 2 + 3 + 1 + 2 + 3 + 1 + 2 + 3 +

5. **2/4**

1 + 2 + 1 + 2 + 1 + 2 + 1 + 2 +

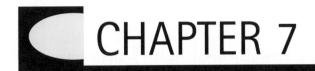

CHAPTER 7

Sixteenth notes: ♬♬

NEW ELEMENT

Rhythm	Term	Value	Rhythm Name
♬♬	four sixteenths	one beat	tika - tika

The *tika-tika* symbol is made up of four stems joined at the top with a double beam. This represents four SIXTEENTH NOTES. Four sixteenth notes are equal to one quarter note or two eighth notes.

To count sixteenth notes using traditional counting, all four subdivisions of the beat need to be indicated. We do this by using the following counting shorthand: "1 e + a." This is pronounced "One-ee-and-ah."

LISTENING   PLAY CD TRACK 49

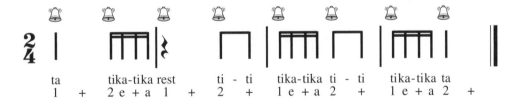

ta	tika-tika	rest	ti - ti	tika-tika	ti - ti	tika-tika	ta
1 +	2 e + a	1 +	2 +	1 e + a	2 +	1 e + a	2 +

PLAY CD TRACK 50

Listen to "Dance of the Toy Flutes" from *The Nutcracker Suite* by Russian composer Pyotr Il'yich Tchaikovsky (1840-1893).

35

TAPPING

🔔 M.M. ♩ = 60

For each of the following exercises, tap the rhythmic pattern with
one hand and the metronome beat with the opposite hand. Then
tap while speaking the traditional counting. In the first two exercises,
the traditional counting has been done for you. For the remaining exercises, write in the traditional counting under the given rhythms.

1.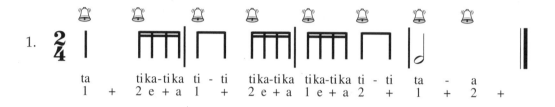

2.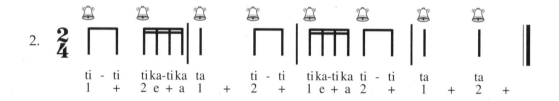

3.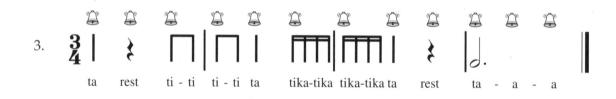

4.

5.

MATCHING

Match the given rhythmic patterns to the boxes shown below, placing them in correct order in the spaces provided. Each exercise is made up of four rhythmic patterns and is played twice. Answers are on page 51.

PLAY CD TRACKS 51

These exercises are in $\frac{2}{4}$ meter.

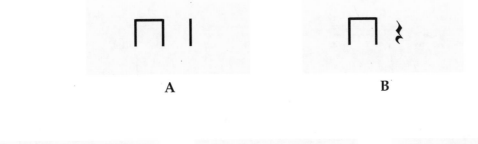

A   B

C   D   E

1. _____   2. _____   3. _____   4. _____

PLAY CD TRACK 52

These exercises are in $\frac{3}{4}$ meter.

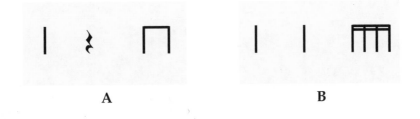

A   B

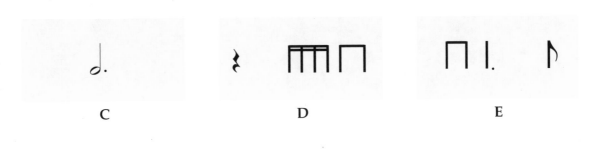

C   D   E

5. _____   6. _____   7. _____   8. _____

DICTATION

Play the tracks one at a time. Write the rhythmic pattern that you hear under the given metronome symbols. Answers are on page 51.

 PLAY CD TRACKS 53–56

1. $\frac{3}{4}$

2. $\frac{2}{4}$

3. $\frac{3}{4}$

4. $\frac{2}{4}$

CHAPTER 8

Pick-up notes and incomplete measures

Until now, we have been working with complete measures—two beats in every measure of $\frac{2}{4}$ meter and three beats in every measure of $\frac{3}{4}$ meter. There are times when you will encounter *incomplete* measures. However, the rules of math still apply. Let's look at the following example.

You will see that the last measure contains only two beats. The missing beat is found in the first measure and is called a PICK-UP NOTE (or ANACRUSIS.) When pick-ups are used, the first and last measures of the piece must always, when added together, be equal to one complete measure in the given time signature. When you add the beats in the first and last measures of the example above, the total is three beats.

When using traditional counting, it is always a good idea to count the missing beats of the first measure. The *tika-tika* are the pick-up notes, and begin on beat three. Note that when there are pick-up notes, the metronome sounds the two missing beats before the pattern begins.

 ## LISTENING   PLAY CD TRACK 57

TAPPING   🔔 M.M. ♩ = 60

For each of the following exercises, tap the rhythmic pattern with one hand and the metronome beat with the opposite hand. Then tap the metronome beat while speaking the traditional counting. You may want to write in the traditional counting before you begin.

From now on, tapping exercises will not include metronome symbols or rhythm names.

1. (exercise notation in $\frac{3}{4}$)

2. (exercise notation in $\frac{2}{4}$)

3. $\frac{3}{4}$ [rhythmic notation]

4 $\frac{3}{4}$ [rhythmic notation]

5. $\frac{2}{4}$ [rhythmic notation]

MATCHING

Match the given rhythmic patterns to the boxes shown below, placing them in correct order in the spaces provided. The metronome will always begin with two count-off beats for the exercises in $\frac{2}{4}$ time, and three count-off beats for the exercises in $\frac{3}{4}$ time. The beat that follows is the beginning of the exercise. If this beat is silent, it means that a pickup note begins the example (thus a shorter rhythm for the first box). Each example will include either four or five boxes. For this matching section, each exercise is a separate track on the CD. Answers are on page 51.

 PLAY CD TRACKS 58–61

These exercises are in $\frac{2}{4}$ meter.

A	B	C	D

E	F	G

1. _____ 2. _____ 3. _____ 4. _____

These exercises are in $\frac{3}{4}$ meter.

A	B	C	D

E	F	G

5. _____   6. _____   7. _____   8. _____

DICTATION

Play the tracks one at a time. Write the rhythmic pattern that you hear under the given metronome symbols. Note that when there is a pick-up note, the metronome sounds the count-off beats, and then the missing beats before the exercise begins. Answers are on page 51.

PLAY CD TRACKS 66–69

1. $\frac{3}{4}$

2. $\frac{2}{4}$

3. $\frac{3}{4}$

4. $\frac{2}{4}$

CHAPTER 9

Eighth-two sixteenth notes:

NEW ELEMENT

Rhythm	Term	Value	Rhythm Name
	1 eighth, 2 sixteenths	one beat	ti - tika

The *ti-tika* symbol is made up of three stems. The last two stems are joined at the top with a double beam. One eighth note and two sixteenth notes have a combined value of one quarter note. When this rhythm is tapped, it will feel like "long, short-short."

From now on, the rhythm names will be shown only for new elements.

 LISTENING   PLAY CD TRACK 70

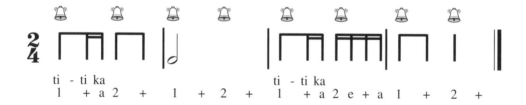

 PLAY CD TRACK 71

To demonstrate this rhythm, listen to an excerpt from the Prelude to Act I from the opera *Carmen* by French composer Georges Bizet (1838-1875).

In all exercises and dictations, it is important to continue tapping the basic beat with the hand opposite the one you use to tap the rhythmic patterns.

TAPPING

🔔 M.M. ♩ = 60

For each of the following exercises, tap the rhythmic pattern with one hand and the metronome beat with the opposite hand. Then try tapping only the metronome while speaking the traditional counting. Finally, try tapping the metronome beat and the rhythm, all while speaking the traditional counting.

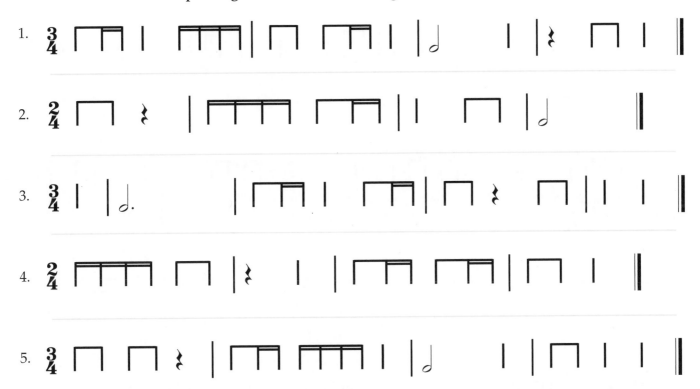

MATCHING

Match the rhythmic exercises from the CD tracks with the boxes given below. Each exercise is made up of four rhythmic patterns. Write your answers in the spaces provided. Answers are on page 52.

💿 PLAY CD TRACKS 72–75

These exercises are in $\frac{2}{4}$ meter.

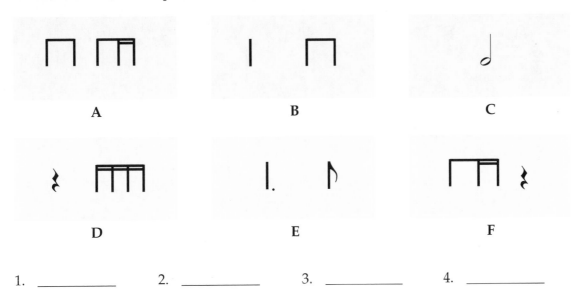

A   B   C

D   E   F

1. _____   2. _____   3. _____   4. _____

Note that when there is a pick-up, the metronome sounds three count-off beats, and then the missing beats before the exercise begins.

 PLAY CD TRACKS 76–79

These exercises are in $\frac{3}{4}$ meter.

A	B	C	D

E	F	G	H

5. _____ 6. _____ 7. _____ 8. _____

DICTATION

Play the tracks one at a time. Write the rhythmic pattern that you hear under the metronome symbols. Note that when there is a pick-up , the metronome sounds a complete count-off measure, and then the missing beats before the exercise begins. Answers are on page 52.

PLAY CD TRACKS 80–83

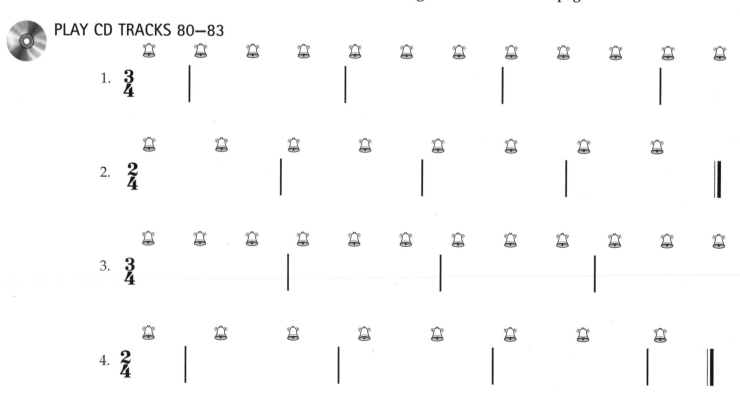

REVIEW TEST

The number of points for each answer is indicated to the left of each question. This first section has a total of 55 points. When finished, check your answers against the answer key on pages 52–53, and tally your score.

POINTS

REVIEW QUESTIONS

1
1. The space between two bar lines is called a _____.

3
2. a) An incomplete measure at the beginning of a piece of music is called a _____ or an _____.

    b) In $\frac{3}{4}$ meter, if the pick-up equals one beat, how many beats will there be in the last measure? _____

2
3. a) What does the top number in a time signature indicate? _____

    b) What does the bottom number mean? _____

1
4. What does a dot after a rhythm symbol mean? _____

2
5. a) What is the rhythm name for this symbol? ♫ _____

    b) How many beats would it receive in $\frac{3}{4}$ time? _____

2
6. How many beats does *tika-tika* represent in $\frac{2}{4}$ time? _____ Write its rhythm symbol: _____

9
7. Write the traditional counting under the following example:

$$\frac{3}{4} \;\; \sqcap\!\sqcap \mid \; | \; \wr \;\; \sqcap \mid \; \downarrow \;\;\; | \; | \; |. \;\; \flat \sqcap \mid \; \downarrow \;\;\; \|$$

20
8. Name the following symbols and fill in the number of beats they would receive in the indicated time signatures. Place an X if the note or rest would not appear in the given time signature. Each blank is worth one point.

Symbol	Rhythm Name	Term	Beats in $\frac{3}{4}$	Beats in $\frac{2}{4}$
♩. ♪				
♩.				
♫♫				
♫				
♩				

5

9. a) If the time signature is $\frac{2}{4}$, how many beats would the following notes or rests receive?

      i. ♩ _____   ii. 𝄽 _____

   iii. ⊓ _____   iv. ❘ _____

    b) Would they have the same value in $\frac{3}{4}$ time? _____

4

10. What are the rhythm names of the following symbols?

      i. 𝄽 _____   ii. ♩ _____

   iii. ♩. _____   iv. ⊓ _____

5

11. If the time signature is $\frac{3}{4}$, how many times would you tap for the following rhythms?

      i. ♩. _____   ii. ❘ _____   iii. ⊓ _____

   iv. ❘. ♪ _____   v. 𝄽 _____

1

12. What does M.M. ♩ = 60 mean? _____

_____

55
TOTAL
POINTS

YOUR SCORE:_____

True progress is built on a foundation of clear understanding.

If your score is 51 or better, proceed with the review dictations on page 47.
If your score is less than 51, review the areas of weakness before proceeding.

46

REVIEW DICTATIONS

PLAY CD TRACKS 84–91

10   1.   **3/4**

8   2.   **2/4**

9   3.   **3/4**

7   4.   **2/4**

10   5.   **3/4**

8   6.   **3/4**

7   7.   **2/4**

7   8.   **2/4**

66 TOTAL POINTS

There is a total score of 66 points for the review dictations.
Check your dictations against the answer key on page 53 and tally your score.

YOUR SCORE:_____

If your score was 61 or better, Congratulations! You may proceed to

RHYTHM WITHOUT THE BLUES VOLUME 2

If your score was 60 or less, you should review any elements
that gave you difficulty before continuing on to Volume 2.

C ANSWERS

CHAPTER 1

MATCHING:
1. B, D   2. A, C   3. C, D   4. B, A

DICTATION:

1.   2.

3.   4.

CHAPTER 2

MATCHING:
1. C, E   2. D, B   3. B, F   4. A, F

DICTATION:

1.   2.

3.   4.

CHAPTER 3

MATCHING:
1. D, B, G, C   2. G, C, A, E   3. C, G, B, E   4. B, E, C, F

5. A, D, E, B   6. D, F, B, A   7. B, E, D, A   8. C, E, D, F

DICTATION:

1.

2.

3.

4.

CHAPTER 4

MATCHING:

1. B, E, A, F   2. A, D, F, B   3. E, C, D, A   4. F, C, E, D

5. D, B, C, F   6. A, E, A, D   7. C, B, F, E   8. F, A, B, C

DICTATION:

CHAPTER 5

MATCHING:

1. F, E, C, B   2. A, E, B, D   3. A, F, E, C   4. F, B, A, D

5. B, H, D, E   6. G, A, C, F   7. A, C, G, D   8. B, D, H, C

DICTATION:

CHAPTER 6

NO EXERCISES

CHAPTER 7

MATCHING:

1. B, E, A, D   2. B, A, E, C   3. E, C, A, D   4. C, A, B, D

5. B, E, D, C   6. A, B, E, C   7. B, A, C, D   8. C, D, A, E

DICTATION:

CHAPTER 8

MATCHING:

1. G, E, A, C, F   2. D, B, A, C   3. F, D, B, E, G   4. A, C, E, B

5. B, E, C, D   6. G, D, B, E, F   7. C, B, E, A   8. G, A, C, B, F

DICTATION:

CHAPTER 9

MATCHING:

1. B, D, E, C   2. B, F, A, B   3. F, E, B, A   4. A, D, F, C

5. G, D, E, A, H 6. E, A, B, D   7. A, C, D, C   8. G, F, C, B, H

DICTATION:

1.

2.

3.

4.

REVIEW TEST

REVIEW QUESTIONS:

1. measure

2. a) pick-up, anacrusis
   b) two

3. a) the number of beats in a measure
   b) which kind of note gets one beat

4. The dot adds exactly half the value of the rhythm it follows.

5. a) ti-tika
   b) one

6. one

7.

8.

Symbol	Rhythm Name	Term	Beats in $\frac{3}{4}$	Beats in $\frac{2}{4}$
♩. ♪	tam-ti	dotted quarter, one eighth	two	two
♩.	ta-a-a	dotted half	three	X
♬♬	tika-tika	four sixteenths	one	one
♪♬	ti-tika	one eighth, two sixteenths	one	one
♩	ta-a	half	two	two

9. a) i. two beats   ii. one beat   iii. one beat   iv. one beat
    b) yes

10. i. rest   ii. ta-a   iii. ta-a-a   iv. ti-ti

11. i. once   ii. once   iii. twice   iv. twice   v. none

12. The metronome will sound 60 times per minute.

DICTATION: